The Medicine Quilt

Inspired by a True Story

Archway Publishing books may be ordered through booksellers or by contacting:

Archway Publishing
1663 Liberty Drive
Bloomington, IN 47403
www.archwaypublishing.com
844.669.3957

Because of the dynamic nature of the Internet, any web addresses or links contained in this book may have changed since publication and may no longer be valid. The views expressed in this work are solely those of the author and do not necessarily reflect the views of the publisher, and the publisher hereby disclaims any responsibility for them.

Any people depicted in stock imagery provided by Getty Images are models, and such images are being used for illustrative purposes only.
Certain stock imagery © Getty Images.

ISBN: 978-1-4808-9216-3 (sc)
ISBN: 978-1-4808-9217-0 (hc)
ISBN: 978-1-4808-9215-6 (e)

Print information available on the last page.

Archway Publishing rev. date: 12/22/2021

Written by Margaret Doom
Illustrated by LaShawn Medicine Horn

"Grown men can learn from very little children
for the hearts of little children are pure.

Therefore, the Great Spirit may show to them
many things which older people miss."

Heȟáka Sápa ~ Black Elk

Dedication

Margaret Zephier
Vince Two Eagles
David Olson

On a great river lined with chalk rock
faces and shedding cottonwoods,

amidst a sea of tall grass seeded with feathered tops,
there was a small town.

In the town, there were those born of that land and those who came to it as strangers long after; between the two groups there was never peace.

Among themselves, they told stories of each other and how they had come to have so much anger between them.

As time passed, the divide grew as wide as the river, and as tall as the grass, rooting deep in the hearts on both sides.

Their anger soaked into the ground until even the earth was hurt by it. The once colorful prairie grew dark under the cloud of hatred that hung over the town.

The animals sensed the earth was no longer full of life and began to flee. The eagles were the first to go, followed by the buffalo and deer, which could no longer drink from the poisoned river.

The crops withered and the jackrabbits fled, until finally, even the coyote disappeared from the hills. Still the people persisted in their hatred of one another, unable to see the loss of life because of the loss in their hearts.

In the little town, there were two Elder women, each from one side of the town's divide. Each had lived on the poisoned land all their lives. They had carried the sadness and anger so long that they grew tired of the burden. Their old eyes saw the anger being passed on to the children.

Finally, because of their love for their people and their desire to help them heal, they came together to talk.

The grandmothers decided to pray for four days. One grandmother went to a hill overlooking the town, the other to a quiet room in her house.

Finally, when the time was over, they met once more. The first grandmother said, "I know that I am very old, and I am afraid the people will not listen to me, but I have had a vision of sewing a great quilt."

The second Grandmother replied, "Yes! I have also had this vision. This quilt could be made of all our love for them, our hope for the future, and the courage we wish to pass on to them! If we sew the quilt with this in our hearts then maybe the people can sit upon it and remember what it is like to live a life full of color!"

The grandmothers gathered the fabric from their homes, tearing apart their own clothing so that they would have enough. Then, together, they went to the very middle of the town to create the quilt. The work was slow as their old fingers threaded the unwilling fabric.

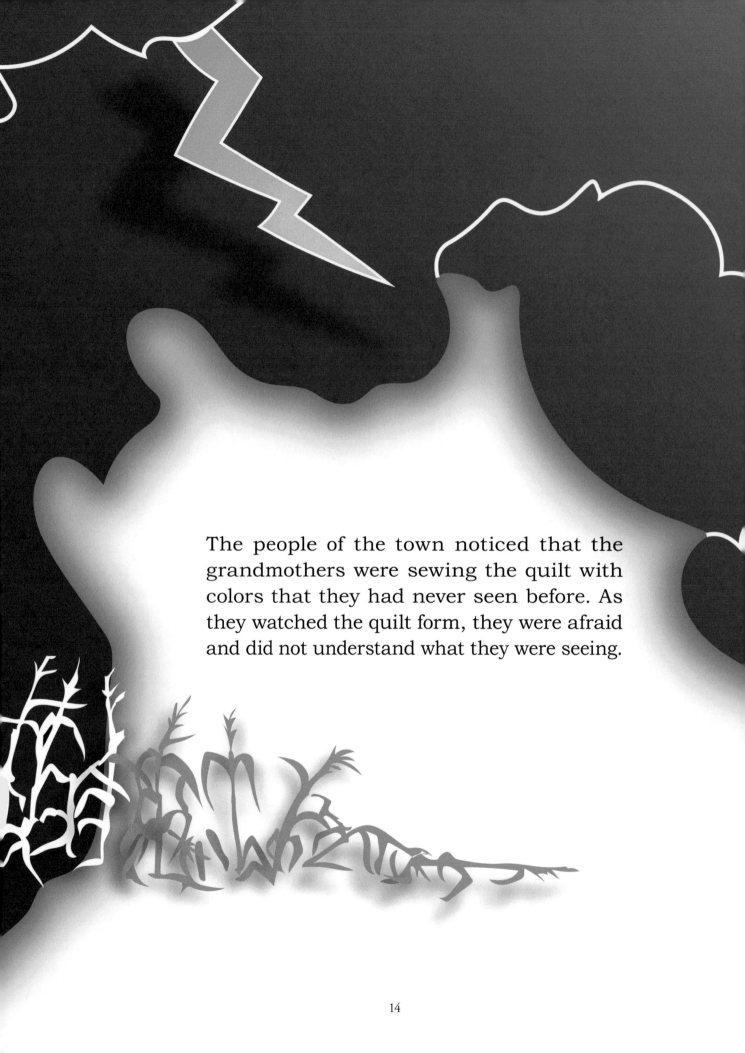

The people of the town noticed that the grandmothers were sewing the quilt with colors that they had never seen before. As they watched the quilt form, they were afraid and did not understand what they were seeing.

The little children of the town, however, were not afraid! They ran to sit at their grandmothers' feet. As they watched, they touched the grandmothers' hands and clung to their dresses. They were delighted by the new colors that the grandmothers were using to sew the quilt.

One of the children pointed
to a patch of color and said,
"Grandmother, I have never seen
this color before! It is so beautiful.
What color is it?" Her grandmother
smiled saying, "That color is love! All
of us need to practice the color of love so that
our hearts become strong". The young girl stood
holding the edge of the quilt out like wings. She began to
dance with excitement. As the quilt rippled and
moved around her the stitches began to form
into butterflies. They spread their wings and
flew from the quilt.

The quilt grew greater and greater until it colored the center of the town. As the people looked at it they remembered somewhere deep inside themselves what it was like when the earth was full of life and color. Cautiously they came to sit upon it. They listened to the grandmothers as they spoke of what had happened in the town. The earth began to stir as flowers grew and blossomed.

The littlest of the children tugged at her grandmother's skirt. She asked in a quiet voice, "Uŋči, this is my favorite one." Her grandmother leaned in and said, "Ah that is a strong color! It is called Courage. It is a color passed down from our ancestors. They help us to feel it in our hearts even when we don't believe it is there."

One young man whose face was tired and sad was amazed and asked, "Grandma, grandma, what is this one?" The grandmother replied gently to him, "That color is hope, my takoža. Hope is for your eyes. When you know what the color of hope looks like, you are able to see far beyond where you are to know that the future will be good." The patch of quilt began to ripple and flow as fresh water poured from the stitches and into the earth.

Another young man walked right up to the grandmothers and said, "I am glad to be here, and I believe this is a beautiful quilt but I do not know what to do. I am afraid of what it might mean to forgive." The grandmothers were both quiet. Finally, the grandmother who had been born of that land stood. Carefully she took the heavy quilt made of fabric from her own clothing and wrapped it around the young man's shoulders. The man began to weep as she spoke, "Much hurt has passed between us, and I too do not know where the path ahead will lead, but we are relatives. We must have the courage to speak truthfully to one another."

As the quilt continued to grow, the people began to practice the colors they saw. Those who were angry wrapped themselves in the color of love. Those who were afraid held on to the color of courage. Those who had despaired that the conflict would never end, touched the color of hope. These colors and many more began to burst forth from the earth as the darkness of anger and mistrust faded.

The river began to flow clean again, inviting the animals to drink from its banks. The grass grew tall, as the cottonwoods lifted their branches in praise of the sky. The deer and jackrabbit, followed by the coyote, and finally the buffalo returned to the land.

Our Contributors

South Dakota Community Foundation

Boys & Girls Club of the Missouri River Area

East River Horizons Inc.

Freeman Network for Peace & Justice

Printed in the United States
by Baker & Taylor Publisher Services